Published by Creative Education
and Creative Paperbacks
P.O. Box 227, Mankato, Minnesota 56002
Creative Education and Creative Paperbacks
are imprints of The Creative Company
www.thecreativecompany.us

Design by The Design Lab
Production by Joe Kahnke
Art direction by Rita Marshall
Printed in the United States of America

Photographs by Alamy (Michele Falzone), Corbis
(Martin Harvey), Dreamstime (Natalija Berg, Lukas
Blazek, Volodymyr Byrdyak, Gsrethees, Honzik7,
Isselee, Iryna Rasko, Jana Šigelová), National Geo-
graphic Creative (ROY TOFT), Shutterstock (kobps2,
Joe Quinn, Serg Rajab), SuperStock (Tier und Natur-
fotografie)

Library of Congress Cataloging-in-Publication Data
Riggs, Kate.
Storks / Kate Riggs.
p. cm. — (Amazing animals)
Summary: A basic exploration of the appearance,
behavior, and habitat of storks, Earth's big wading
birds. Also included is a story from folklore explaining
why marabou storks have featherless heads.
Includes bibliographical references and index.
ISBN 978-1-60818-758-4 (hardcover)
ISBN 978-1-62832-366-5 (pbk)
ISBN 978-1-56660-800-8 (eBook)
1. Storks—Juvenile literature.
QL696.C35 2017
598.3—dc23   2016004916

CCSS: RI.1.1, 2, 4, 5, 6, 7; RI.2.2, 5, 6, 7, 10;
RI.3.1, 5, 7, 8; RF.1.1, 3, 4; RF.2.3, 4

First Edition HC 9 8 7 6 5 4 3 2 1
First Edition PBK 9 8 7 6 5 4 3 2 1

AMAZING ANIMALS

STORKS

BY KATE RIGGS

CREATIVE EDUCATION • CREATIVE PAPERBACKS

Milky storks live in Cambodia and Indonesia

Storks are birds with long legs. They wade through water and tall grasses. There are 19 kinds of storks in the world. They live on many islands and all **continents** except Antarctica.

continents Earth's seven big pieces of land

A bill sticks out from a stork's face. Some bills are long and curved. Other stork bills are shorter and flatter.

An Asian openbill stork (left);
a marabou stork (above)

The small Abdim's (right); the large marabou (opposite)

Storks are big birds. Abdim's stork is the smallest **species**, though. It is 10 times smaller than a marabou stork. The marabou stork is the largest stork. It is about 5 feet (1.5 m) tall and weighs 20 pounds (9.1 kg).

species a group of similar (or closely related) animals

Most storks like to live near water. They are usually found in streams and ponds. They walk carefully through swamps. Some storks live in drier grasslands or forests.

Painted storks wade through wetlands to find food

A saddle-billed stork feeds on fish as well as frogs and crabs

A stork grabs food with its bill. It eats frogs, fish, **insects**, and worms. Some storks use their bills to open shells. They can eat snails and clams then. Storks do not have teeth. They use their bills to tear up their food.

insects small animals with three body parts and six legs

A female stork lays two to six eggs. The mother and father stork keep the eggs warm. Then **chicks** come out. They have fluffy feathers called down at first. New feathers grow, and chicks start to fly. They leave the nest when they are about two months old.

chicks baby storks

A wood stork can live about 18 years in the wild. White storks may live 25 to 30 years. Young storks must watch out for **predators**. But adult storks do not face as many threats.

predators animals that kill and eat other animals

A see-through inner eyelid
keeps a stork's eye clean

Storks have excellent eyesight. They can spot **prey** when it moves. They grunt and hiss to each other. Sometimes storks clack their bills. They let each other know if they are mad or scared.

prey an animal that is killed and eaten by other animals

People who live in the southern United States might see wood storks. Watch quietly as these huge white birds move through the water!

Wood storks are the only storks that have their babies in North America

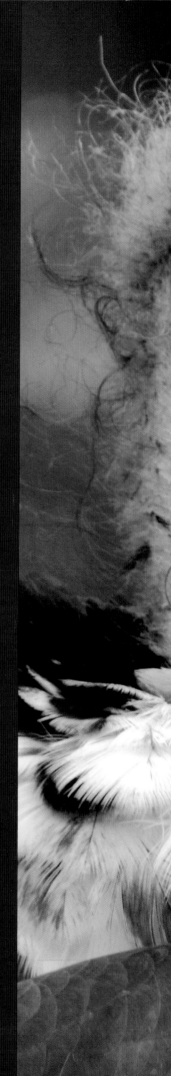

A Stork Story

Why is the marabou stork's head featherless? People in Africa told a story about this. Hyena once had a bone stuck in his throat. He was choking and needed help! Marabou Stork stuck his head into Hyena's mouth. As Stork grabbed the bone with his bill, Hyena's jaws shut! Stork freed his head, but all his feathers were left to tickle Hyena's throat. Hyena still laughs.

Read More

Collard, Sneed B., III. *Beaks!* Watertown, Mass.: Charlesbridge, 2002.

Stewart, Melissa. *Feathers: Not Just for Flying.* Watertown, Mass.: Charlesbridge, 2014.

Websites

National Geographic: Wood Stork
http://animals.nationalgeographic.com/animals/birds/wood-stork/
Listen to the sound a wood stork makes, and learn more about these birds.

San Diego Zoo Animals: Stork
http://animals.sandiegozoo.org/animals/stork
Check out pictures and fun facts about storks.

Note: Every effort has been made to ensure that the websites listed above are suitable for children, that they have educational value, and that they contain no inappropriate material. However, because of the nature of the Internet, it is impossible to guarantee that these sites will remain active indefinitely or that their contents will not be altered.

Index

bills 7, 12, 19
chicks 15
eggs 15
eyesight 19
feathers 15, 22
homes 4, 11, 20

kinds 4, 8, 16, 20, 22
nests 15
predators 16
prey 12, 19
sizes 8
wading 4, 11